MW01716579

Dr. Mao's

SECRETS OF FERTILITY

Hundreds of Natural Ways to Increase Your Fertility and Health

By: Dr. Mao Shing Ni

Library of Congress Cataloging-in-Publication Data available.

Designed by Laurie Dolphin Design © 2011

Second Edition 2012

Reprint March 2022

www.askdrmao.com

. . . .

Note to Readers:

This book is intended to provide helpful and informative material and is provided with the understanding that the author and publisher are not engaged in rendering medical, health, or any other kind of personal professional services in this dictionary. Natural remedies and supplements can have side effects, both alone and in combination with other remedies or conventional medicines. The user of this book should consult his or her medical, health, or other competent professional before adopting any of the suggestions in this book or drawing inferences from it. The author and publisher specifically disclaim all responsibility for any liability, loss, or risk, personal or otherwise, which is incurred as a consequence, directly or indirectly, of the use and application of any of the contents of this book.

Statements contained herein have not been evaluated by the food and drug administration. These products are not intended to diagnose, treat, cure or prevent disease. Always consult with your professional healthcare medical provider before changing any medication.

. . . .

Table of Contents

Introduction

The first step toward parenthood begins with your inner wish to have a child. Whether you have just begun to hope for a child, or whether you have been trying for some time, Secrets of Fertility will help prepare your mind, body, and spirit for this journey.

This book offers a simple holistic approach for getting pregnant, using the time-tested wisdom of the East. The 5,000-year-old Eastern medical tradition emphasizes treating the whole entire person—mind, body, and spirit—rather than just the part that isn't functioning well. In the case of fertility, Western medicine would typically focus on just the reproductive system, while Chinese medicine would assess a woman's whole body and lifestyle, creating tailored treatments designed to bring the woman to an optimal, balanced state of health. The best treatments for promoting fertility work with a balanced integration of Western and Eastern medicine—which is why this book incorporates the best advice from both medical systems.

In the following pages, you will discover natural tips to increase your chances of conception: nutrition, herbs and supplements, environmental considerations, special fertility-enhancing exercises, stress-reduction techniques—and even a 28-

day fertility plan that is based on traditional Chinese medical treatments for promoting fertility. All of these tips will help you create a fertile ground for your future baby.

Let us begin by learning the three key principles of Chinese medicine, which form the basis of this book.

Principle 1: The body is a holistic whole

The first principle of Chinese medicine is that the body is more than just a collection of parts; it is a whole organic entity, with many different systems working together in concert. When all bodily systems are working together harmoniously, you enjoy optimal health. Therefore, when one system is being treated, all other systems must be considered as well, or everything will fall out of balance. The dietary, herbal, supplemental, exercise, and lifestyle tips in this book will bring every system in your body to a state of balanced health, while still having a powerful effect on your fertility potential.

Principle 2: The body has a relationship with nature

Chinese medicine holds that the human body has a relationship with nature. As humans, we are members of nature, and nature supplies the energy we need to thrive and survive. The changes in nature—including the passage of seasons, weather, natural disasters, and manmade environmental influences—will directly or indirectly affect our lives and impact our state of health. You will find out in Chapter 2 how to best work with these environmental influences to enhance your health and fertility.

Principle 3: Humans have a relationship with their created communities

This brings us to the third principle, which is that humans have a relationship with the societies they create. As social creatures, we often interact with others and are affected by our created communities. Our interactions with one another affect us all, resulting in a wide variety of emotional reactions. The emotions we experience of joy, sadness, anger, or grief can create imbalances in our body and health. It is of critical importance to manage your stress and emotions when trying to conceive. Chapter 6 will give you plenty of restorative techniques and positive guidance to bring you in close touch with the root of your emotions—and with your relationships.

Keeping these three important principles in mind, Chinese medicine encourages women to become responsible and take authority over their own health. In fact, in China, where patients are often responsible for keeping their own medical records, the patient and doctor work together as partners in health. Ideally, you should be able to personally understand your state of health so that you can start taking the necessary steps to improve your odds of conception. Many women have improved their chances of fertility and maintained a healthy pregnancy by following the guiding principles of Chinese medicine, sometimes in combination with Western medical advances. The point is that you should work with your doctor, but ultimately, you are in the driver's seat when it comes to taking responsibility for your health. Only you know what your body has been through in life, and only you have the power to implement the health changes that will pave the way to successful conception.

The 28-Day Plan to Fertility

Taking these principles one step further, this book begins with an outline for a 28-day plan to fertility—your program for fertility-enhancing foods, exercises, and spirit-lifting techniques that you can do every day during your cycle to improve your chances of conception. Using traditional Chinese wisdom for fertility as a guiding force, this program helps you become attuned to the changing needs of your mind, body, and spirit during your monthly cycle.

Deciding to become a parent is one of the most important decisions you will ever make. Any journey you take requires preparation, and this book offers you the secrets to fertility that will get you ready. I am very honored to share tips for achieving maximum fertility. Secrets of Fertility is your roadmap to better health, and may it serve you well on your way to a happy, giggling baby!

Chapter 1

28 Days to Fertility

At my practice, women seeking fertility practice a 28-day program that is designed to optimize their fertility potential through a careful selection of foods, exercise, and spiritual reflection. Nourishing your physical and spiritual bodies is essential in helping you prepare yourself for conception. Since the length of the ideal menstrual cycle runs twenty-eight days, regulating it is the single most important task you face when trying to get pregnant. Your menstrual cycle, which loosely corresponds to the lunar cycle, is composed of multiple separate-yet-interconnected processes, which must happen in order for you to become pregnant. Chinese medicine views these cycles much like the four seasons: Menstrual (cleansing), follicular (growth), ovulatory (peaking), and luteal (withering).

Menstruation: First 3–7 days

The day your menstruation begins is the first day of the approximately 28-day cycle. This phase can be likened to the hibernating and quiet energy of winter. During this phase, your uterine lining sheds, while your uterus contracts and is cleansed. The quietude of female hormone activity is similar to the quietude of winter.

Follicular: 5–10 days

Just like springtime signals the sprouting of new energy and life, this phase marks the beginning of the new fertility cycle. It is the time between menstruation and ovulation when follicles gradually grow until one stands out.

Ovulatory: 3–5 days

In the way that summer is in full bloom, this phase marks the moment when the follicle grows to its maximum size and maturity before releasing its egg. The luteinizing hormone (LH) works in concert with the follicle-stimulating hormone (FSH), while estrogen increases. The surge of hormones signals the ovaries to release the egg but begins the process of nourishing the uterine lining to provide a receptive place for the embryo.

Luteal: Final 12–14 days

As the leaves begin to fall and the temperature drops, the final shedding of leaves and branches occurs. During this phase between ovulation and menstruation, the uterine lining continues to build up before the final shedding in menstruation.

To simplify matters, we can pair these four phases into two by combining the menstruation and follicular phase. This will take us to the first phase of the 28-day fertility program. This phase starts on the first day of your period and continues through the fourteenth day, before ovulation. The second phase will begin on the fifteenth day and should be continued until your period recommences. Eat a wide variety of whole foods, rather than one or two that you like best, to ensure better nutrition for your body. All foods should be organic; the reason for this is that the chemicals in conventionally grown food can disrupt your endocrine function and decrease fertility.

TIPS FOR EACH PHASE

Phase One: Days 1–14

For the first two weeks, your meals should include foods that will strengthen your egg quality and increase your energy, or qi in Chinese medicine. Whole grains and high-protein foods like eggs, meat, and beans will comprise most of your meals. Refrain from consuming raw foods because they require more energy for digestion. If you feel weak and look pale, consume hot and warm foods like soup, beef, chili, stews, and warming root vegetables like beets and turnips. At this time, it is crucial you avoid cold and icy foods.

Exercise should also be incorporated into your program; intensity will depend on your energy levels. If you have strong menstrual cramps, a more strenuous activity like brisk walking and biking is actually healthier, but only during cramping time. It is best to avoid jumping, pounding, running, or going upside down. This could potentially cause retrograde menstruation where the menstrual flow goes upward through the fallopian tubes and into the pelvic cavity instead of flowing downward through the cervix and out the vagina, potentially creating inflammation throughout your body, such as endometriosis. This phase is a cleansing time where you are gaining a new opportunity to conceive again. When you aren't cramping, engage in exercises that are gentle or only moderately strenuous, such as tai chi, qi gong, yoga, pilates, or swimming.

A helpful visualization practice is to use the "Golden Light" for warming and radiating energy throughout your womb. Start by sitting comfortably on a chair or a cushion on the floor, and breath naturally and slowly. Clear your mind of all thoughts and focus on growing the Golden Light in your abdomen starting at an acupoint called Guan Yuan—or the Gate of Origin; then expand the light with each inhalation until it permeates your ovaries and fallopian tubes on both sides of your pelvis, as well as your uterus. Continue with this meditation for at least 10 minutes, and do it twice a day.

During this cleansing phase, nourish your mind with positive thoughts. Place images of healthy babies and happy families around you, and each day, begin by saying a positive affirmation about your health and fertility that is personal to you, ten times in a row.

Phase One: Sample Breakfast Meals

During the first phase, the warming breakfasts listed below will assist in the cleansing process. Eat a different one each day, and be sure your ingredients are organic.

A note about soy milk: The recipes below often call for soy milk. However, if you have thyroid problems, substitute with almond milk, or even better—goat or sheep's milk. Soy contains phytoestrogen, which can help women who are low on estrogen and experiencing difficulty with pregnancy.

- 1 cup of warm oatmeal + 1 cup warm milk or organic unsweetened almond milk + handful mixed berries + sliced half banana, sprinkled with cinnamon + 1 cup hot green tea
- 1 cup warm quinoa + handful of mixed walnuts, cashews, and almonds + 1 cup hot green tea
- 3 pieces of lightly toasted whole grain bread + 2 tablespoons of nut butter + 1 teaspoon fruit preserves + 1 cup warm milk or unsweetened soy milk
- 3 warm blueberry waffles lightly drizzled with fresh maple syrup + beverage of 1 cup warm unsweetened soy or cow's milk

- 1 cup whole-grain granola + 1 cup unsweetened yogurt + 1 cup warm chocolate-flavored soy milk

Phase One: Sample Lunch and Dinner Meals

For each lunch and dinner, vary the organic vegetables, grains, beans, and protein in one of these combinations:

- 1 medium-sized chopped yam or sweet potato sautéed in broth + steamed kale + light topping of sesame oil
- 1 cup cooked brown rice + 1 cup cooked black beans + sautéed or steamed squash or zucchini
- 1 cup cooked millet and/or quinoa + 4 ounces of sautéed tofu + diced tomato + chopped green onions

Phase Two: Days 15–28 (or the first day of your period)

After the initial cleansing phase, you will transition into a renewal phase. At this time your uterine lining builds up and starts to secrete mucus to moisten and attract the fertilized egg. The lining starts to rise and creates spaces for egg implantation. During this phase, you will need to consume foods that will help to improve the lining, mucus production, and blood flow. Berries and leafy greens like spinach, kale, and Swiss chard will keep your blood running smoothly. As before, it is best to refrain from eating icy, cold foods.

Exercise in moderation and avoid jumping, running, and any other activity that will promote retrograde menstruation. Yoga, pilates, qi gong, and meditative practices are suitable. The gentle exercises in Chapter 5 are particularly helpful at this time.

Be sure to get at least 8 hours of quality rest at night and everyday practice ten minutes of meditation. You can try the Stress Release Meditation in Chapter 6: Less Stress for Greater Fertility.

Phase Two: Sample Breakfast Meals

Again, making sure ingredients are organic, eat one of these breakfasts every day of the second phase:

- 1 large poached egg + 1 slice ham or turkey + 2 slices toasted whole-grain English muffin + 1 6-ounce glass of freshly squeezed orange juice
- Protein Shake: Blend 2 cups unsweetened soy milk + half of a banana + 1 teaspoon wheat germ + 1 teaspoon almond powder + handful of berries on the side
- 2-egg omelet + spinach, mushrooms, and tomatoes + 6-ounce glass of freshly squeezed orange juice
- 1 chicken sausage + 2 slices of tomato + 4 slices avocado + 1 slice toasted whole-grain bread with non-dairy spread + handful of berries on the side

- Egg and turkey sandwich: 1 scrambled egg + 2 slices hormone and nitrate-free turkey breast + 1 slice of tomato + 3 slices avocado sections + blanched spinach + whole-wheat English muffin
- 4 to 5 ounces of soft tofu scrambled with zucchini, green onions, mushrooms, and leafy greens of your choice + whole grain tortilla wrap + 1 cup soymilk
- 2 large scrambled eggs + diced green onions and garlic + sandwiched with 2 slices of lightly toasted whole-grain bread + 1 tablespoon olive oil as topping + 6-ounce glass of freshly squeezed orange juice

Phase Two: Sample Lunch and Dinner Meals

For each lunch and dinner, vary the organic vegetables, grains, beans, and protein in one of these combinations:

- 4 to 5 ounces of baked or roasted wild Alaskan salmon + 1 cup cooked grain (quinoa, brown rice, barley, or sorghum) + sautéed spinach
- 3-ounce sliced organic turkey breast + 1 cup of mashed yams + 1 cup of mixed green beans, or snow peas and carrots + a half cup of sliced papaya for dessert
- 1 cup of steamed sliced beets + salad of mixed greens, handful of unsalted sunflower seeds and walnuts + half of a

sliced avocado + shredded chicken + half a cup organic grapes for dessert

- 4 to 5 ounces of sirloin steak + sautéed kale + a half cup of organic cherries or berries for dessert
- 1 cup of whole-grain pasta topped with a half cup of freshly made meat sauce + steamed or sautéed winter squash and carrots + side of sautéed Swiss chard

Chapter 2

Seasonal and Environmental Factors

Your external environment impacts your internal environment, influencing your health and wellbeing. Engaging in activities that calm your spirit, simplify your lifestyle, put you in tune with nature, and protect your body from toxins will contribute to increased quality of life, which translates to enhanced fertility. For example, taking a power nap in the afternoon will refresh and rejuvenate you, lowering your risk for heart disease and stroke, and essentially telling your body it is safe to become pregnant.

A healthy lifestyle also reduces the likelihood that your bad genes will get expressed. This is an important element in the nature versus nurture equation. Nature refers to natural law, or your genetic makeup, while nurture refers to what people do to facilitate nature.

For example, a mother feeds and nurtures her baby to help him or her grow.

Chinese medicine has always emphasized the importance of being attuned to your surroundings to promote wellbeing. The environment influences your mood, bodily function, and physical energy. Seasonal changes, weather, and time of day all play an important role in your health, and therefore your fertility. Additionally, we live in a modern society that is replete with toxins, and although we can't completely avoid them, we can certainly decrease our exposure to them. Reducing the use of chemically-laden beauty products, cookware, and pesticides, while surrounding yourself with a supportive and uplifting community will contribute to your wellness and fertility.

Cock's Crow Occurs Only in the Morning

You may find better success with conception if you make love in the morning rather than at night. This discovery has been known for a few thousand years by Chinese medicine and is now being embraced by the scientific community based on recent studies in China. So many couples force themselves to copulate at the end of the day when the energy of both people is at the lowest point in the 24-hour cycle. Additionally, the body's hormonal system is naturally at its lowest point by nighttime. It takes energy to spark the conception and what better time is there than after a good night's rest, particularly if you haven't stayed up all night trying. A free bonus—a man's sperm count is highest in the morning—not to mention his natural erection!

Timing is Everything

It is important for the egg and sperm to connect at the most opportune moment. Therefore, sexual intercourse is best performed on the day of ovulation. This is the time during your cycle when the ripened egg is released from the ovary and travels down the fallopian tubes to the uterus. You may also have sex every other day starting approximately one week before ovulation each cycle. One of the most accurate ways to target your ovulation is by taking your morning basal body temperature (BBT). A female's non-ovulating temperature is between 96–99 degrees Fahrenheit. However, when the egg is released, the temperature rises about half a degree and remains slightly elevated until right before menstruation.

Charting your temperature for several cycles can help you become more aware of your ovulation. Stress, lack of sleep, and alcohol may all affect your temperature. For an accurate reading, you must have at least three hours of uninterrupted sleep. You can find more about taking your BBT in Chapter 7. Another method to check when you are ovulating is to examine your cervical mucus. For a few days after menstruation, your mucus may be dry or sticky. When your cervical mucus becomes somewhat clear, slippery, and stretchy—like a raw egg white—this is when you are most fertile.

Spring and Summer Loving Bring Fertility

According to the rise and fall of the energetic polarity of yin (female) and yang (male) in Chinese medicine, male and female fertility is affected by season. During the spring, male energy buds, climaxing around the summer solstice on June 21. Female energy begins to grow in autumn and reached its apex around the winter solstice on December 21. Therefore, female fertility is strongest during autumn and winter, while male fertility is stronger during the spring and summertime. Studies conducted in China have confirmed an abundance and mobility of sperm production during spring and summer. Conversely, the ovaries are more active and produce more follicles during fall and winter. One possible explanation is that because men are generally more physically active during spring and summer, growth hormone and testicular function increase accordingly. Since ovulation occurs ideally at a lowered body temperature, the cooler fall and winter months are more conducive to female fertility. It is important to note that fertility decreases at too high of a temperature. When body heat rises above 98.6 degrees and environmental temperature is overly hot, there appears to be a drop in male testicular function and a delayed maturation of female follicles.

Stoke the Fire of Life in Your Belly

A successful conception and pregnancy are often influenced by circulation and the temperature in one's belly. The most critical part of the human body is in the abdomen, which is also where the reproductive system is located. It is an unfortunate fact that most people do not keep their abdomen sufficiently warm and well circulated. An example of this negligence is exhibited by the fashions that expose the belly or shrink the waist; this clothing leaves the belly vulnerable to cooler temperatures and cuts off circulation. It is no wonder more women are having increasing difficulties with fertility. To keep your belly fire stoked, be sure to keep your abdomen warm by massaging it and layering clothing over it.

Nurture Nature

Our environment plays a large role in our overall health and fertility. A serene environment can foster tranquility and peace, which leads to a strengthened immune system and increased fertility. A beautiful beach, park, or mountain panorama can rejuvenate and nourish your mind, body, and soul. An increase in vitality will bring an increase in your fertility. So step outside, feel the grass between your toes, bask in the daylight, and take some quiet time in nature!

Let the Sunshine In

There is some evidence that the amount of exposure to light affects a woman's menstrual cycle and ovulation. In addition, studies indicate that there is a link between less light exposure and increased depression. Depression fosters less fertility, so try to expose yourself to natural or full-spectrum light during the day. Sunlight is also an excellent natural source of vitamin D, which studies show plays an important role in fertility. Vitamin D helps produce testosterone, which is the hormone responsible for sperm production. In women, vitamin D helps regulate how estrogen is used to help egg follicles mature and grow. To protect your skin from sun damage, it is best to go out before 10 am or after 3 pm and wear sun protection.

Stop Smoking: No Butts About It!

Tobacco adversely affects your lungs, increases your risk for cancer, and decreases your chances of fertility. A study published in the journal Fertility and Sterility demonstrated a 17% lower sperm count in male smokers than non-smokers. On the flip side, the same journal published a study showing an increased sperm count of 800% for those men who quit smoking. Beware of second-hand smoke, which can be just as hazardous to your health and chances of getting pregnant. For a healthy body and baby kick the habit and go smoke-free!

Eliminate Mercury

Mercury is a naturally occurring metal that has several forms and is increasingly found in our food sources and environment. When it is combined with other elements, it forms inorganic mercury compounds. It combines with carbon to make a common compound called methylmercury, which is produced mainly by microscopic organisms in soil or water. This methylmercury, which may be formed in water, accumulates in the tissues of fish. Larger and older fish tend to have the highest levels of mercury. If you consume seafood that is contaminated, the mercury in your body passes to the fetus. The mercury can also be passed on to your infant through breastfeeding. Brain damage, mental retardation, coordination issues, blindness, seizures, and inability to speak are all potential side effects of methylmercury consumption. Children poisoned by mercury may develop neural and digestive problems, along with kidney damage. If you prefer to consume fish, choose wild Alaskan salmon and refrain from seafood high in mercury like tuna, swordfish, tilefish, King mackerel, and shark. Nearly all shellfish also contain traces of mercury so limit your intake. The FDA and EPA say pregnant women may safely consume up to 12 ounces a week of two average-sized portions of salmon, Pollock, cod, and catfish. For more information, you may visit www.epa.gov/waterscience/fish.

Natural Beauty for Fertility

Our skin is the largest organ in our body and therefore absorbs everything we put on it like a sponge. Just as consuming whole, organic foods is important to fostering fertility, applying only safe, mild, organic products to your skin is essential. Many commercial creams, shampoos, and lotions contain harsh chemicals that seep into our skin and into our blood. These chemicals may disrupt hormonal balance and potentially cause cancer and decrease fertility. If you normally color your hair, it would be a good time to stop doing so when trying to conceive. Make sure to read the ingredients on the products and avoid the following ingredients: parabens, mineral oil, paraffin, petroleum, sodium lauryl or lauryl sulfate, propylene glycol, phenol carbolic acid, dioxane, toluene. Look for 100% organic products with USDA certification stamp.

Cleanse Your Kitchen of Toxins

How you cook and store your food may influence your fertility as much as what you eat. Researchers have found chemicals called perfluorinated compounds (PFCs) might be linked to impaired fertility. PFCs are often found in Teflon non-stick cookware and have been shown to damage the pituitary gland. The pituitary gland secretes hormones that regulate growth, reproduction, and many metabolic processes. Another harmful chemical found in plastic, packaged food, and beverages is BPA (Bisphenol A). Heating or freezing plastic may cause dioxins from the plastic to leach into your foods. Therefore, store your food in glass or ceramic containers and do not microwave in plastic or foam. Instead, choose cast-iron and ceramic cookware to be chemical-free and increase your fertility.

Chapter 3

Nutrition for Fertility

Proper nutrition is an essential component in helping you increase fertility. Like a flower needs the sun, water, and healthy soil to thrive, we need the right nourishment to build a healthy foundation to conceive. Processed foods are not only detrimental to our health, but they also decrease the likelihood of fertility. Our bodies absorb nutrients more efficiently through whole foods like vegetables, fruits, legumes, whole grains, nuts and seeds, healthy fats, and proteins. Countless studies have confirmed the healing power of food that contains disease-fighting compounds that improve organ function and support overall health.

During pregnancy, your body is experiencing tremendous changes as it prepares to create a new human being. Therefore, it is crucial to consume the best-quality nutrients to help equip you and your child for healthy development. A good place to start is to evaluate your overall eating patterns, so you can replace old bad habits with healthier ones that will maximize your fertility. The healthier you are, the healthier your baby will be, so start with good habits now. A great way to keep track of your daily food intake, and motivate yourself to make healthier choices, is to write down what you eat in a food journal.

Once you take your eating habits into perspective, you may begin to rethink grocery shopping and concentrate on healthier items. In addition to reevaluating your eating habits, food safety is also an important factor to ensure a healthy and safe environment for you and your future baby. Eating well and feeling well is an essential foundation for a healthy pregnancy and a healthy child.

Live Food Gives New Life

The medical tradition of China—well-known as the most populous people in the world—has long considered certain foods valuable in increasing success with fertility. These fertility foods include eggs, nuts, seeds, beans, legumes, and berries. Since these foods are themselves capable of propagation when hatched or sprouted, they are said to be abundant in life-giving energy. These complete foods provide the essential amino acids that help form the building block of protein. They are also high in essential fatty acids (EFAs), critical for hormonal health, and chock full of antioxidants that prevent a premature decline in function and aging.

Balance is Key

In our practice, we always stress the importance of balancing the five food groups, which is a traditional Chinese medical plan includes: vegetables, fruits, beans, grains, and meat. (Dairy is not usually a part of the traditional Chinese medicine food program, though it can be included sparingly.) Not only do all five food groups need to be met every day, but all colors should be eaten every day. Taking vegetables as an example, every day you would want to eat: green leafy vegetables, orange veggies like sweet potatoes, red beets or tomatoes, white mushrooms, and dark veggies like eggplant. Consuming a wide variety of foods and colors is essential; favoring only one type of food can cause imbalance, or even malnourishment—bad news for your fertility.

Eat a Rainbow of Fruits and Veggies!

A study published in OBGYN News found that nearly 80% of infertile couples had a lower-than-average intake of fruits and vegetables, which are abundant in disease-fighting antioxidants and healthy fiber. Supplying your body with a wide spectrum of nutrient-rich foods is essential for building a healthy foundation for fertility. Most vitamins, minerals, and antioxidants contained in fruits and vegetables work synergistically, giving your body the nutrients it needs to enhance your health and fertility. Therefore, make sure to eat your rainbow of antioxidant-rich fruits and veggies—a recommended seven to nine servings every day. Keep in mind that one serving is about one cupped palm's worth of food, less than many people think!

Fertility Gains with Whole Grains

One of the essential five food groups, grains are complex carbohydrates that supply energy; they are rich in vitamins and minerals, cholesterol-free, low in fat, and high in fiber. We require more servings from the grain group than any other group. The grain group includes two subgroups: whole grains and refined grains. Whole grains are far more nutritious than refined grains. All grains begin as whole grains. In their natural state growing in the fields, whole grains are the entire seed of a plant. This seed, or kernel, is made up of three key parts: the bran (the outer coating), the germ (the embryo), and the endosperm (the largest portion of the kernel). The refining process normally removes the bran and the germ, leaving only the endosperm. Without the bran and germ, about a quarter of a grain's protein is lost, along with fifteen or more key nutrients. Your best whole grain choices are whole wheat, brown rice, amaranth, quinoa, barley, sorghum, triticale, and oats.

Make Room for Fiber

Fiber has a host of health benefits that range from cholesterol reduction to blood sugar improvement while promoting regularity. The healthier your body and digestion are, the higher the chances are to improve fertility. Fiber also increases satiety by adding bulk to your food, but without the added calories. Because fibrous foods take longer to digest, you will get a slow release of sugar into your bloodstream, keeping you satisfied over a longer period of time. Thus, balanced blood sugar levels and satiety will prevent your sneaky sugar cravings! Foods that are particularly high in fiber include apples, bananas, pears, berries, oranges, dried plums, broccoli, peas, artichokes, avocados, kale, oatmeal and oat bran, barley, brown rice, beans and legumes of all kinds, almonds, flax seeds, and sunflower seeds.

Ripen Your Fertility with Raspberries

While all berries have antioxidant properties that benefit health, the raspberry stands alone as a fertility booster. Not only does the raspberry improve egg quality, but it also stabilizes blood sugar, brightens your eyesight, and strengthens your uterine lining. It can relax the uterus, as well, helping prevent miscarriages. Raspberries are among the plants with the highest known fiber content, and nutritionally are a good source of iron, magnesium, and manganese. As an additional bonus, raspberries help improve and beautify your skin. Raspberry leaves, which are sometimes prepared as a tea, contain vitamins B1, B3, and E, all of which help promote a healthy pregnancy.

Go for Goji Berries

Considered an herb-grade food in Chinese medicine, goji berries can easily be used in your everyday meals. Rich in antioxidants, vitamin C, B1, and B2, these bright orange-red berries are effective in male and female fertility treatment. Goji berries stimulate the uterus to thicken the lining, an important step in fetal implantation. For men, goji berries also help strengthen follicular quality and improve sperm count within one or two months. They help balance blood sugar metabolism and for this reason, are often employed to treat hypoglycemia. Goji berries are also very beneficial for both a healthy mood and vision support. Sometimes the dried berries are steeped as a tea. Goji berries can be found at your local health food store. Sprinkle a handful in your salad, add to your trail mix, or toss a handful in your cereal for a sweet and healthy meal!

Consider Calcium

As the most abundant mineral in your body, calcium is essential for proper heart, muscle, and nerve function, as well as bone formation. Calcium also plays an important role in follicular production and general reproductive functions in both men and women. The best source of calcium is, of course, dairy products, but other sources include dark leafy greens, broccoli, orange juice fortified with calcium, beans, and sardines. If you are intolerant or allergic to dairy, then non-dairy sources are a better alternative for you, since allergies and intestinal disturbances may interrupt proper endocrine function, negatively affecting fertility potential.

Fertility with Folate Foods

Folate, or folic acid, is a B vitamin that is especially important before and during the first months of your pregnancy, helping to prevent anemia and neural tube deficiencies. Folate also boosts egg quality, improving your chance of getting and staying pregnant. In addition, folate helps the fetus develop normally, and decreases the risk of malformation of the spine, brain, and skull. While a daily supply of 400 micrograms of folate suffices for most women, the recommended dietary allowance for those trying to conceive is 600 micrograms per day. Your prenatal vitamin will supply you with this amount, but you may also want to consume dark leafy greens like kale, broccoli, spinach, beet greens, turnip greens, bok choy, asparagus, legumes, beans, peas, sunflower seeds, oranges, melons, and fortified whole grains.

Choose the Right Fats

Not all fats are created equal, so choose heart-healthy fats that will improve your health and increase fertility. Avoid trans fats that lower your good cholesterol and increase your bad cholesterol. Read the ingredients listed on packaged foods and avoid any products that contain "partially-hydrogenated" fats. Trans fats are usually found in margarine, shortening, and any product that has a long shelf life. Eat red meat, butter, and animal fat in small quantities, especially if you are predisposed to increased cholesterol. This fat can burden your liver and interfere with estrogen production; it can also impair endocrine system function and your ability to develop normal, healthy embryos. On the other hand, monounsaturated and polyunsaturated fats, such as vegetable, nut, and seed oils, increase good cholesterol and protect you from heart disease, inflammation, and premature skin aging. These include olive oil, rice bran oil, walnut oil, flaxseed oil, peanut oil, and sesame oil. It is best, however, to not cook with these oils; instead, use as salad dressings or drizzle on top of already cooked dishes.

Go Fish!

The DHA and EPA omega-3 essential fatty acids found in fish reduce inflammation, maintain healthy brain function, and are vital for fetal brain and eye development. Reduced inflammation in the pelvic area may facilitate getting pregnant more easily. Since the oil of fish improves blood flow, it may help improve uterine lining development and promote blood flow to the ovaries. For whole fish, choose wild Alaskan salmon, and refrain from seafood that tends to be high in mercury like tuna, swordfish, tilefish, King mackerel, and shark. The FDA and EPA say pregnant women may safely consume up to 12 ounces a week or two average-sized portions of salmon, Pollock, cod, and catfish. Vegetarian sources of omega-3 can be found in flaxseeds, walnuts, and algae. If you choose to take fish oil, be sure it is high quality, with a USP (United States Pharmacy) certification, which indicates a reduced amount of mercury in the oil.

Protein Keeps Fertility on Track

Protein is essential for muscle and tissue formation. Eggs and lean meats like chicken and turkey breast, lamb, and veal contain essential fatty acids, vitamins, minerals, and amino acids that are necessary for reproductive function. In addition, these foods are an excellent source of iron, which is essential for both preventing anemia and increasing fertility potential. Red meat, including beef, lamb, and pork, contains essential nutrients like iron, protein, and zinc, requirements for healthy growth and development and overall wellness; in spite of these benefits, red meat should be eaten in moderation. Try to consume only hormone- and antibiotic-free meats to further increase your chances of getting pregnant.

Vegetarians and Fertility

If you are a vegetarian, you may lack certain nutrients that you can't always get from eating plants alone. You may supplement your diet with a B complex, particularly B6 and B12, which are very important for fertility. B9 (folic acid) is also critical before and during pregnancy for proper fetal development, especially of neural tubes. Make sure to include adequate protein found in nuts, seeds, beans, legumes, and nut butters. Protein is essential for muscle and tissue formation, so include a serving at every meal and snack.

Healthy Weight for Fertility

Carrying insufficient or excess weight is not conducive when pursuing the goal of motherhood. Obesity reduces the chance of pregnancy and can cause gestational complications for the mother and child. Dieting isn't a healthy strategy either; your focus should be geared toward attaining a healthy weight and getting an optimal array of nutrients. Certain guidelines like the BMI (body mass index) may help you determine whether or not your weight is within a healthy range. In general, a BMI below 18.5 is considered underweight, 18.5–24.9 is normal weight, 25.0¬–29.9 is overweight, and anything over 30.0 is considered obese. To calculate your BMI, divide your weight in pounds by your height in inches squared, and then multiply that sum by 703. For example, if you weigh 150 pounds and are 5'5 (65 inches), then the following calculation would apply: (150÷65x65) x 703 = 24.96. You may also speak with your doctor to help you better understand your healthy BMI.

Don't Skip Meals: Eat Your Way to Fertility

If you fall into the habit of skipping meals, you may prevent yourself from achieving a healthy weight and healthy blood sugar levels. The timing of meals is just as important as what you eat.

Skipping meals sets your body into starvation mode. As a result, your body will hold onto every calorie longer while decreasing your metabolic rate dramatically. That is why you must eat food, so that your body stays in the habit of burning it up. As a general rule of thumb, try not to go more than 3.5 or 4 hours without a meal or snack.

Say No to that Cup o' Joe

An occasional cup of coffee to give you a lift will probably not make or break your fertility potential. However, because caffeine is a stimulant, overconsumption may chronically stimulate your nervous system. Drinking coffee every day temporarily raises your blood pressure, increases your heart rate, and compromises your blood sugar levels. This could stress your adrenal glands, which might then impair the function of uterine contractions, tubal functions of transporting the egg, and implantation itself. If you already drink coffee, cut back to less than one cup daily, and if you are over the age of 35 it is best to not drink coffee at all.

A Drink a Day Keeps Fertility Away

Drinking alcohol has been shown to decrease fertility potential in both males and females. Alcohol affects your liver's health, which has a close relationship with female and male sex hormones. Alcohol can create an imbalance in your hormones, and ovulation may become irregular. For your male partner, alcohol can damage the structure, speed, and liveliness of sperm. In addition, drinking alcohol increases the risk for miscarriage, preterm birth, stillbirth, and other serious conditions. So, instead of drinking spirits, lift them with a relaxing massage or a happy tune!

Sugar-Free for Fertility

Much like a car runs on fuel, the human body requires sugar for energy. Natural, whole-food sources like fruits, whole grains, and milk can provide us with this necessary fuel. However, overconsumption of sugar, especially added refined sugars can impair our health. When we eat sugar, the pancreas is called upon to produce and release insulin, a hormone that empties the sugar in your bloodstream into all the tissues and cells for usage. Overindulging in sugar can elevate insulin levels. Chronically raised blood insulin levels beyond the norm can lead to a depressed immune system, and decreased proper ovarian function. Excess sugar may create more acidity in your cervical mucus, which is less conducing for sperm retention and production. It can also reduce sperm motility in men, making it more difficult to reach the woman's egg. Additionally, most of the excess sugar is stored as fat in your body, which results in weight gain and elevates the risk for heart disease and cancer.

Cut Out the Salt

Excess salt intake may elevate blood pressure and promote water retention. These excessive intracellular fluids can weaken reproductive system function, decreasing fertility. So hold the salt when cooking and savor spices and herbs to flavor your food instead. Take extra caution when dining out, as most restaurants tend to cook with too much salt. Watch for condiments and sauces, which tend to be a swimming pool of salt. Be a savvy shopper and make sure to check the sodium content on the nutrition facts label. All of the nutrition information listed on the label is per serving; if the sodium is higher than 5% per serving, stay away. Some spices and herbs to try are garlic, cinnamon, sage, Chinese 5 spice, ginger, cloves, curry, cumin, oregano, rosemary, and fennel. Make the most of your meals and health by spicing it up!

Eat Dark Chocolate

You don't have to wait for Valentine's Day to savor chocolate! Cocoa contains potent antioxidants that may protect against LDL oxidation—bad cholesterol. It may even lower blood pressure and minimize the blood's ability to clot, hence reducing the risk for strokes and heart attacks. Chocolate can lift your spirit due to its content of phenylethylamine, which is a slight antidepressant and stimulant that is similar to your body's own adrenaline. Cocoa may also increase serotonin and thus contribute to a positive mood. Happiness means less stress and more fertility. Make sure to consume chocolate with a cocoa content of at least 72%. For maximum benefits enjoy 1 ounce of dark chocolate about three times per week—but no more.

Drink Green FertiliTEA!

Rich in the antioxidant EGCG (epigallocatechin gallate), green tea has multiple health benefits ranging from inhibiting cancer cell growth to improving cognitive function, cardiovascular health, and eye health. Healthy cholesterol improves microcirculation, which is important to the development of both your eggs and uterine lining. Green tea does, however, contain caffeine, so drink no more than two cups of green tea daily and only one cup a day during pregnancy. On another note, don't take your prenatal vitamin with green tea, as the phytates in the tea may prevent the absorption of calcium and iron in the vitamin. It is best to wait several hours to drink tea after taking your prenatal vitamin.

Drink Filtered Water

Water is a vital beverage for good health. Like planet Earth, our bodies are comprised of 60 to 70% water. Our body needs water to help us metabolize and digest the food we eat. Each and every cell needs water to perform its essential functions. Eight 8-ounce glasses of water a day is the usual recommendation. However, the kind of water you drink makes a difference. It is best to choose filtered or bottled water. Studies show that tap water is filled with contaminants, antibiotics, and a number of other unhealthy substances; consider investing in a quality carbon-based filter for your tap water. On the go? Try using a stainless-steel thermos or glass bottle, filled with filtered water. Make sure that the water isn't too icy because your body uses precious energy to warm it up. This energy and circulation can be used instead in your pelvic area, uterus, and your ovaries. If you are tired of the same old plain water, spruce it up with a refreshing infusion of basil, fresh lemon, mint leaves, and a drop of honey.

Purge Your Pantry

To improve your diet and by extension, your chances of fertility, clear your kitchen of processed foods, soda, and other unhealthy foods. Artificial colors, flavors, and preservatives should be eliminated from your diet. These chemical, toxic additives can weaken your endocrine and other internal systems, which can decrease your body's ability to cleanse itself. They may also interfere with your metabolism and the conversion of hormones. Read your food labels, and get rid of anything that contains: MSG, BHA/BHT, sugar in its many forms, artificial sweeteners, trans fats, sodium nitrate, olestra, food colorings, potassium bromate, and generally anything that you can't pronounce! Remember, what harms your health harms your fertility.

Go Organic

Your body should be a healthy nest for your child, not a breeding ground for harmful pesticides, chemical fertilizers, and hormones. All of these additives create a chemical burden and toxic environment, making it more difficult to conceive. If you don't have access to organic foods, be aware of which fruits and vegetables are the highest and lowest in pesticides. The Environmental Working Group (EWG) is a nonprofit organization dedicated to environmental investigations and can be a great source of information. Most pesticides reside in the skin of fruits and vegetables, so at the very least, peel the skins if you can't purchase organic. Look for a USDA label on products to ensure they are 100% organic. Try to consume hormone- and antibiotic-free dairy, meat, and poultry, whenever possible.

Keep Your Food Safe

Viruses or bacterial infections may impair your chances of fertility so take precautions to ensure food safety. Be sure to wash raw fruits and vegetables thoroughly before consuming them. You may soak them in a bath of cool water, add a splash of vinegar, and scrub the skins to remove any debris. Handle raw meats, poultry, seafood, and eggs carefully, and use separate knives and cutting boards for them. Thoroughly clean any utensils and cutting boards that have touched raw meats with hot water and soap. Thaw meats and fish in the refrigerator and don't eat any perishable foods that have been left unrefrigerated for more than two hours. Cooking your food well can help kill harmful parasites and bacteria. When eating in restaurants, avoid foods that may have bacterial contamination, including sushi, salad bars, buffets, unpasteurized beverages or food products, and raw or undercooked meat, poultry, fish, and eggs. Store foods at low temperatures, below 40 degrees F to minimize bacterial growth. Remember to wash your hands with warm soap and water for at least thirty seconds before eating. For a complete list of food safety guidelines, you may visit www.cdc.gov/foodsafety.

Chapter 4

Fertility Herbs and Supplements

Herbs have been prevalent in every culture and medical tradition since the earliest humans walked on earth. Huge volumes of books about healing plants and substances have been compiled by medical practitioners, from the philosopher-physicians of China to the Vedic doctors of India, the physicians of ancient Egypt and Greece, and the medicine men of the Americas. Chinese herbal medicine is one of the oldest, most systematized, and most researched natural healing systems in the world. Treating fertility with herbs is often used in Chinese medicine as a complementary or primary step. In addition to herbs, supplements may support our health when the body is lacking certain nutrients. Although the best way to get your nutrients is through a well-rounded diet consisting of whole foods, sometimes taking supplements can enhance your health. Therefore, in addition to consuming a healthy diet, your prenatal vitamin may provide you with added support for your developing baby.

Whenever possible, use supplements that are extracted from whole foods like fruits, vegetables, and grains. These will have the best bioavailability, meaning the highest absorption by your digestive system. The best way to take vitamins and minerals is in powdered form, liquid concentrate, or oil. Avoid taking mega-doses or any dose larger than the recommended dietary allowance (RDA) of any nutrient, no matter how good they may be for your health. Before deciding to take any herbs or supplements it is best to consult with your physician and healthcare practitioner to avoid any drug interactions or contraindications. Many herbs and supplements must be discontinued with pregnancy.

Start with a Prenatal Vitamin

A prenatal vitamin is designed to provide you and your developing baby with specific nutrients. It is similar to a multivitamin except that prenatal vitamins contain more iron, calcium, folic acid, and vitamins A, C, and D. Look for a prenatal vitamin that is USP (United States Pharmacy) certified. While taking your prenatal, use precaution with other supplements; you want to prevent overloading on any one nutrient. Also, look for prenatal vitamins that do not contain added supplements and herbs.

Enhanced Fertility with Fish Oil

Fish oil is comprised of EPA and DHA fatty acids, which balance your cholesterol and reduce inflammation. DHA, in particular, is essential for fetal brain development; so in addition to your prenatal vitamin, it is wise to supplement with high-quality fish oil. Less inflammation in your body results in reduced pelvic inflammation, which can help you get pregnant. Fish oil also improves blood flow, which can help promote uterine lining development. Make sure your fish oil supplement is USP (United States Pharmacy) certified, which ensures a reduction of mercury and pesticides in the product.

The Conception Connection: L-carnitine and L-arginine

Derived from the amino acid lysine, L-carnitine is essential to energy metabolism and the anti-aging process. L-arginine helps to optimize the function of the endocrine system. These two amino acids work synergistically to enhance the egg quality and improve blood flow for uterine lining development. They work most effectively if taken during the time when you are trying to conceive, and should be discontinued once you are pregnant. You can look for these as supplements, or eat foods that are rich in these amino acids. Find L-carnitine in beef, bacon, and other pork products, tempeh and other fermented soy products, whole milk and other dairy products, and avocados. Good sources of L-arginine include nuts, seeds, eggs, meat, poultry, seafood, soybeans, chickpeas, and oatmeal.

Remember to choose antibiotic-free, grass-fed, organic foods, whenever possible, to lessen the toxic load on your body.

Think Zinc

This essential trace element plays an important role in neurological function, immune response, and growth and development. Zinc affects female fertility by promoting proper cell division, which is critical to the earliest stages of conception and fetal development. Studies indicate that zinc can also increase semen and testosterone production in men. Adequate zinc intake assists in the absorption of folate, a critical B vitamin necessary for fetal development and the prevention of anemia. Zinc also helps transport vitamin A through the blood. Elemental iron supplementation—though not dietary—levels of 38–65 milligrams per day may interfere with zinc absorption. Dairy, chicken, eggs, enriched grains, beef, almonds, cashews, chickpeas, peanuts, and baked beans are good dietary sources of zinc.

For Him: Prostate Health with Selenium

A healthy prostate is essential to increase male fertility. Studies indicate that the trace mineral selenium appears to inhibit cellular changes that lead to prostate cancer. Selenium is a component of the antioxidant enzyme glutathione peroxidase, which protects tissues from oxidative damage caused by free radicals. Low plasma selenium is associated with up to a 5-fold increased risk of prostate cancer. Since plasma selenium decreases with age, it is important to ensure you are eating enough in your diet; Brazil nuts, seafood, enriched brewer's yeast, and grains are all rich sources. Although the recommended dietary allowance (RDA) is 55 micrograms, most research was based on a daily intake of 200 micrograms.

Herbal Help for Fertility

While the herbs that follow are often used by traditional practitioners to promote fertility, each individual has different needs, and that is why it is best to work with a licensed traditional herbal practitioner who can tailor the herbal formula to your specific needs. When a practitioner creates a formula, he or she bases the herbal ingredients on your constitution, your environment, and your medical condition. A typical formula usually contains ten to fifteen herbs. It is possible that you can find some of these herbs as supplements in your local health food store, but these herbs often work synergistically with one another and may be less effective on their own. If you are serious about enhancing your fertility naturally, working with a licensed traditional herbalist can be a powerful way to improve your overall health and jumpstart your fertility potential. You may find a licensed practitioner on www.acupuncture.com.

Fertility Boost with Morinda Root

Morinda root is the root of a wintergreen shrub that has traditionally been associated with benefiting the sexual activities of men. In addition to improving thyroid function, Morinda root is effective in treating fertility. It stimulates the blood circulation around the uterus and increases the implantation rate. Traditionally used as a muscle and tendon strengthener, it may also mitigate menstrual symptoms such as dull lower abdominal pain, back pain, and cold painful limbs. While improving blood flow to the uterus, it treats gestational musculoskeletal aches and pains and may decrease the risk of miscarriage. Morinda root is also used to treat male infertility accompanied by signs of premature ejaculation and low libido. Often found with other herbs in libido- and performance-enhancing formulations for both women and men, it is available in health food stores, sometimes under the pharmaceutical name Radix Morindae Officinalis, online, and from acupuncturists and Chinese herbalists.

Cleanse and Circulate with Cistanche

Cistanche is a major herb used in Chinese herbalism. It treats infertility and at the same time, it also helps promote regularity, cleansing the body of wastes. Additionally, cistanche is used to alleviate the side effects of losing blood and nourishment during menstruation. Cistanche increases male vitality and fuels the necessary sexual fire while improving blood circulation and hormonal release in the female uterus. During the proliferation phase of the female cycle, it improves progesterone efficacy. As a result, cistanche indirectly promotes the thickening of a woman's uterine lining, which provides a greater chance for implantation. Sometimes called Herba Cistanches, this herb can be found online through herb suppliers or at the offices of Chinese medical practitioners.

Stoke Sexual Fire with Horny Goat Weed

Thousands of years ago, Chinese shepherds noticed that goats, after eating a certain weed, would become sexually energized and active. The weed was epimedium, also known as horny goat weed. Historically used for its treatment in sexual dysfunction and infertility, this herb increases sperm production. It also stimulates sexual desire in men and women, referred to as "stoking the fire within", by Chinese medicine. This herb has been shown to strengthen male and female libido by increasing testosterone production, as well as corticosterone and cortisol. Lab tests demonstrate blood pressure reduction with this herb by dilating the coronary arteries. It also facilitates increased oxygen circulation, decreased cholesterol, and a strengthened immune system. Also called Herba Epimedii, horny goat weed is available in health food or vitamin stores, online, and from Asian pharmacies and acupuncturists, many times in a formula with other natural libido-boosters.

You can find horny goat weed combined with other herbs in our Infinichi formulas Spark Male, which brings male sexuality into satisfying natural harmony and encourages natural function, as well as Spark Female, our formula that increases a woman's libido.

Got Milk Vetch Root?

Milkvetch root, also called astragalus, is a well-known tonic herb in Chinese medicine that promotes the health of the immune system and strengthens the body against disease. This root is effectively used in reproductive medicine, especially in cases of anemia, chronic fatigue conditions, frequent cold and illness, hypothyroidism, inadequate uterine lining development, and postpartum recovery. Current research is testing its effect on enhancing insulin sensitivity and treating insulin resistance in patients with polycystic ovarian syndrome. One way to take it is to place one or two pieces of the dried root in a teacup, pour boiling water over it, and enjoy as a tea. Milkvetch, also called astragalus or Radix Astragali, can be found in Asian specialty stores and at the offices of Chinese herbalists.

You can find milkvetch root combined with other herbs in our Infinichi Immunity, which helps defend against colds, flu, and respiratory tract infections.

Regulate Your Cycle with Chinese Angelica Root

This powerful herb has been used in Chinese medicines for thousands of years to help regulate women's menstrual cycles. The

Chinese name "dang gui" means "should return" which is very fitting, as it helps regulate a woman's cycle. It fulfills this action by increasing blood flow to the uterus. Chinese angelica root alleviates menstrual pain by facilitating the shedding of the uterine lining before and during menstruation. In addition, it helps increase estrogen during menopause, when there is often a large decline in estrogen production. Anemia, insomnia, and other sleep disorders have also been treated with angelica root in combination with other herbs. It may also be found under the name dang gui, dong quai, or Radicis Angelicae Sinensis; look in herbal specialty stores, in Asian markets, and in the offices of Chinese medical practitioners.

Angelica root is frequently combined with other herbs to solve feminine issues and increase blood circulation. If you are interested, you can find this herb combined with other herbs in our Wellness Living formulas:

- Pain is used to relax muscles and soothe pain.
- Passages Plus helps women cope with the hormone swings of PMS and menopause.
- Fire Core Element Capsules helps promote blood flow to nourish the heart and brain.

Chinese Foxglove Root Replenishes Blood Production

Considered one of the most important herbs for treating infertility in Chinese medicine, Chinese foxglove root, also called rehmannia, helps a woman during menstruation by nourishing various hormonal aspects of the blood. This root works very well in synergy with Chinese angelica root to support the ovaries, hormone production, thickening of the uterine lining, and follicular development. If signs of anemia arise, it helps by increasing red blood cell production. Since this herb is so effective in blood nourishment and replenishment it is often described as an anti-aging herb. Chinese foxglove—also called Radix Rehmanniae Preparata or simply rehmannia—can be found through herb suppliers or at the offices of Chinese medical practitioners.

You may find Chinese foxglove root combined with other herbs in the following Wellness Living formulas:

- Sleep calms the spirit, alleviates insomnia, and increases the body's ability to cope with stress.
- Spark Male brings all the components of male sexuality into satisfying natural harmony and encourages natural function.
- Metal Core Element Capsules enhances immunity.

Chinese Dodder Seed: Beneficial for Him and Her

This powerful herb boasts a bounty of benefits for men and women. It is primarily used as a male sexual tonic to treat impotence, premature ejaculation, nocturnal emission, frequent urination, and to reduce abnormal sperm chromosomal issues. For women, it strengthens egg quality, induces better ovulation, and treats vaginal discharge. Chinese dodder seed also helps thicken the uterine lining, very beneficial for women with elevated follicle-stimulating hormone (FSH) levels and women who respond poorly to IVF or intrauterine insemination (IUI). Chinese dodder seeds, sometimes under their pharmaceutical name Semen Cuscutae, can be found online through herb suppliers, at some health food stores, or at the offices of Chinese medical practitioners.

Hormonal Support with Asian Cornelian Cherry

Asian cornelian cherry, sometimes called cornus berry, is the fruit of the dogwood tree. This tart, small sour cherry is helpful in cases of excessive urination and uterine bleeding. It supports the hormonal component of blood and is often used to treat infertility. The astringent quality of the cherry holds the period to full term; it also supports the fertilized egg in holding onto the uterus, reducing the risk for miscarriage. Asian cornelian cherry is sometimes used to treat insomnia that accompanies hormonal deficiencies. Be like the empresses of China and drink a tea made of Asian cornelian cherries. Just drop 7 to 10 berries into a teacup, pour boiling water over them, and drink once the tea is cool. You can find Asian cornelian berry dried, in tinctures, powder and capsule form, sometimes under the name Fructus Corni; look in Asian specialty stores, online, or at the offices of Chinese herbalists and medical practitioners.

Chinese Yam Enhances Endocrine Function

A delicious ingredient in soups and bean dishes, Chinese yam is a food-grade herb that contains multiple health benefits. It assists the pancreatic enzymes of food digestion and helps regulate blood sugar levels. It has been used in China for hundreds of years to treat diabetes, and current research confirms Chinese yam's effect in modulating blood glucose fluctuations. It is therefore effective for those with prediabetic symptoms and blood sugar sensitivities. Chinese yam also strengthens endocrine function and is ideal for enhancing female fertility. As a delicious and mild-acting herb, it can easily be introduced into your diet. This herb is usually available in its dried and sliced form and can be taken as a tea. It can also be used in cooking. If your recipe involves a short cooking time, soak the dried wild yam for a couple of hours before adding. Chinese wild yam can be found in ethnic food stores, through online herb suppliers, or at the offices of Chinese medical practitioners; it is sometimes found under its pharmaceutical name, Rhizoma Dioscoreae.

You can find Chinese wild yam combined with other herbs in the Wellness Living formulas that may be helpful support for your overall health and fertility:

- Water Core Element Capsules reduce the effects of a stressful lifestyle and enhance stamina and reproductive health.
- Passages Plus helps women cope with the hormone swings of PMS and menopause.

Maca Root: Strengthen the "Master Gland"

A Peruvian root-like vegetable grown in high altitudes, maca root has been used by native Peruvians for thousands of years in food and medicine to promote fertility, endurance, energy, vitality, and sexual virility. Maca helps to nourish the endocrine system and strengthen the pituitary gland, referred to as the "master gland." The pituitary controls hormone functions, governing our body temperature, thyroid activity, and growth during childhood, urine production, testosterone production in males, and ovulation and estrogen production in females. Take note that maca is very high in iodine and those with thyroid disorders should be cautious. Speak with your healthcare provider to determine the right dosage and to see if maca is appropriate for you. It should be discontinued once you get pregnant.

Chaste Tree Berry Brings Balance

Also known as vitex, this Western herb helps regulate periods and controls excessive menstrual flow. It is also helpful in treating those individuals with elevated levels of prolactin or male hormones, restoring hormonal balance. Prolactin is secreted by the anterior pituitary gland that is located in the midbrain area. Although prolactin is necessary to stimulate milk production in the mammary glands, too much prolactin can disrupt ovulation and your menstrual cycle. Chaste tree berry is most often taken as a tincture, though the dried berry may also be ground and sprinkled on food or into a drink.

Chaste tree berry, or vitex, can be found in health food stores, online, and at the offices of herbalists.

Sleep Tight with Supplemental Support

Adequate sleep and inner peace is essential for overall and reproductive health. You can promote restful sleep with the herb valerian, used for hundreds of years to treat insomnia, menstrual cramps, anxiety, and nervous headaches. Valerian is available in capsules or tincture form and may be taken one hour prior to bedtime. Speak to your healthcare provider to determine the appropriate dosage for you. Schizandra berry calms the spirit and takes the edge off anxiety. Its berries are often made into a tea. For better quality sleep, I often recommend to my patients my Sleep Formula, which calms the spirit, alleviates insomnia, and increases the body's ability to cope with stress.

Another substance that can help is melatonin, a naturally occurring hormone that is produced by our pineal gland. Melatonin is produced in your body to regulate your circadian rhythm, the inner clock for your sleep cycle. Whole foods containing melatonin include oats, rice, ginger, tomatoes, turkey, tofu, milk, nut butters, and potatoes. A typical dosage is 0.1 to 0.3 milligrams one hour before bedtime. Discontinue once you become pregnant.

Chapter 5

Exercise and Rejuvenation Practices for Fertility

The benefits of exercise on your cardiovascular health are well documented. In addition to preventing diseases like diabetes, exercise boosts energy, promotes a healthy weight, balances organ function, calms your mind, and increases your overall longevity potential. It improves your circulation and helps your blood flow to various areas of the reproductive system. During my many years of clinical practice, I have studied the habits of centenarians and something they all had in common was that they led physically active lives. Many centenarians I encountered practiced the gentler mind-body exercises tai chi and qi gong, which have always been associated with health and longevity. These exercises are especially beneficial for decreasing stress and increasing fertility. By deliberately activating the flow of energy and removing blockages, communication is restored and organ functions return to their optimal level.

In conjunction with exercise, the Chinese energy communication system of acupuncture is also effective for fertility. By stimulating and activating certain meridians, or energy points, in the body, you can elicit certain physiological responses. If you do not have access to acupuncture, you can perform self-applied acupressure, which follows the same principles as acupuncture. Instead of needles, you use your own fingers to stimulate specific points on your body that will enhance your reproductive health.

Make Time to Exercise

Exercise benefits your health in multiple ways, especially when you are trying to conceive. It improves circulation and stimulates your endocrine glands to secrete hormones necessary for reproduction. Progesterone and estrogen hormones improve the quality of the egg while regulating the menstrual cycle. Regular exercise helps to regulate your endocrine system, thereby improving your chances of fertility. Moderate exercise like gentle cycling, a well-paced walk, or thirty minutes of other moderate aerobic activity is ideal. The best exercises focus on breathing and strengthening your body such as yoga, tai chi, and qi gong. During pregnancy, it is best to avoid jumping and any other strenuous activity, which can potentially cause retrograde menstruation or deplete your energy.

You may choose prenatal yoga as another option for a more gentle, yet excellent form of physical activity.

Release Your Emotions

Many people store their emotions in the body instead of releasing them through healthy outlets. This may eventually manifest as chronic pain in the back, neck, shoulders, stomach, and jaw area. Unexpressed emotions may also cause shortness of breath, chest tightness, and result in decreased fertility. When the nervous system is affected, your hormones and reproductive health can suffer as a result. Tai chi, yoga, meditation, exercise, massage therapy, artistic outlets, or qi gong are all effective ways to help you unleash negativity so you can prevent illness and boost your fertility.

Try Qi Gong

Qi gong is a series of traditional Chinese exercises that have been passed down for thousands of years. The gentle exercises focus on breathwork and meditation. They have been helpful for individuals suffering from arthritis, autoimmune disorders, and cancer. Qi gong helps you feel revitalized and peaceful as it directs energy to help nourish your body internally. The fertility-enhancing qi gong exercises that follow are ten meditative poses that should be practiced in order twice each day. It is best to practice qi gong after waking and before bedtime, and never on a full stomach. Wear lightweight, comfortable clothing. A quiet, peaceful environment is suitable for this practice, as it will allow more tranquility for your emotions and mind. Breathe slowly and deeply, and as you become more familiar with the exercises, you can close your eyes.

Pose 1: Gathering the Essence of the Universe

Ready to begin? Start by holding each pose for 1 minute and work your way up to 3 minutes for each pose. Stand with your feet shoulder-width apart, knees slightly bent, arms and hands held out in front of you as if you are hugging a small, inflated balloon. Your fingers are relaxed and your palms are facing your pelvic area. Close your eyes and imagine that you are attracting a balloon of heat into the space just in front of your pelvic area.

Pose 2: Arousing the Fire

In the same standing posture as pose 1, bring your hands to your pelvic area and press gently. As you do this, imagine that the balloon of heat is being pressed into your pelvis, warming up the area all-around your pelvis.

Pose 3: Anchoring to Mother Earth

Sit in a chair with your feet shoulder-width apart, allowing your legs and feet to naturally relax. With your back gently erect, place your palms softly on your knees. Tilt your chin down, as if letting your eyes focus on your knees, but keep your eyes closed. Imagine that your palms are full of warmth, heating your knees as the energy travels down toward the sides of your feet.

Pose 4: Gathering the Energy of Love

On either a clean floor or a somewhat firm bed, sit in a gentle cross-legged position, also known as the lotus position. If this position is uncomfortable for you, continue to sit in a chair as in pose 3. On each hand, let your middle finger and thumb touch, with the ball of your thumb gently placed over your middle fingernail; this is known as the hand pose of compassion in many Asian meditative practices, which integrates the heart with the spirit. Visualize a wave of loving feeling and compassion overflowing into your body.

Pose 5: Tending the Circles of Life

Continue sitting cross-legged, with your spine gently erect. Bring your palms to your pelvis and gently press. Breathe slowly, without any undue force. Imagine the warmth from your palms radiating into your ovaries. Visualize your ovaries smiling like a smiley face.

Pose 6: Relaxing the Three Spheres

Relaxing the three spheres alludes to relaxing your mind, body, and spirit. Lie down, on the floor or bed, with both legs straight and shoulder-width apart. Relax both arms at your sides with palms facing upward. Take an inhalation, and during each exhalation, visualize every single cell and muscle in your body relaxing, from the crown of your head to the tips of your toes. Move down your body, mentally relaxing each part of your body in order, from your head, face, neck, shoulders, chest, stomach, pelvis, lower back, and buttocks, to your thighs and upper arms, to your legs and lower arms, and downward to your feet and hands.

Pose 7: Descending the Fire

Similar to pose 2, you are now lying down instead of standing. Lie down with both feet spread about shoulder-width apart, and allow your body to completely relax. Put a soft pillow underneath your knees if it is more comfortable. Bring your hands to the front of your pelvis. With your elbows on the floor or on the bed, place your palms so they are facing your pelvis. Again, visualize a small balloon of warm air in this space between your palms and your pelvis. The warm air penetrates your pelvis.

Pose 8: Compressing the Fertile Garden

Bend your knees, and bring them upward toward your pelvis. Grab your left hand with your right hand, creating a lock on your knees and legs. You will feel some pressure in the front of your hip joints and possibly your pelvis. This pressure should be noticeable but not painful. Imagine your abdomen flattening and your hips relaxing more with each exhalation. This should bring your knees slowly and naturally closer to your pelvis. Breathe deeply and slowly. This pose creates pressure in your reproductive area through your pelvis, especially the fallopian tubes and the upper part of your uterus, increasing stimulation and blood flow into the area.

Pose 9: Opening the Gate of the Phoenix

Continuing from pose 8, bring your arms down on both sides of your body with palms facing upward. Allow your bent knees to gently open to either side. The hands assume the hand pose of compassion. As you breathe slowly and naturally, imagine a wave of loving feeling and compassion overflowing in your body. This pose will help you relax your cervix and the lower part of your uterus.

Pose 10: Opening the House of Conception

Bring your legs down, bending your knees, allowing your thighs to open, and letting the soles of your feet touch each other. Take care that you allow your knees to fall naturally to either side without any undue force. Assume the hand pose of compassion and place the back of your hands on the crease where your thighs meet your genitals. Imagine that the inside of your uterus is like the floor of a tropical rain forest: mossy, warm, damp, and rich with nutrients and all the ingredients for life. Any seed that falls onto this floor will germinate. This pose relaxes your entire reproductive system and allows it to open up.

Self-Help Acupressure

Acupressure uses the same principles as acupuncture to unblock your body's energy meridians. Stimulating and activating certain acupoints in the body's energy communication network can elicit specific and intended physiological responses. Acupuncture and acupressure are very beneficial to fertility and for your overall health. Acupressure helps you release endorphins, reduce stress, reset your circadian clock, and balance your endocrine system. Certain points in your body are connected via this network to your reproductive health, which can be massaged and stimulated twice a day. The four points that follow may help you boost your fertility.

Press Here to Awaken Your Endocrine System

The first point is called Kidney 1, or Overflowing Well. This point is located on the sole of your foot and when stimulated, it can awaken your nervous and endocrine systems. In Chinese medicine, it is referred to as an overflowing well because this is where the energy of the body flows to the surface. It also benefits fertility by improving circulation and blood flow to your pelvic area. As a result, the quality of your egg may be improved. To find the point, cup your foot in your hand with your sole facing you. Mentally divide your foot into three sections. If your heel is the first part and your toes are third, the second part is the area that lies right behind the metatarsal joint—in the center of your sole. Place your thumb—the right thumb if you are right-handed and the left if you are left-handed—squarely on this spot. Place your second thumb next to the first and press down with firm pressure, wrapping your other fingers around your foot to give you leverage for applying pressure. Press firmly to permeate through the thick soles of your feet, then release. Repeat this pattern for one minute on each foot.

Gather Your Female Energy with Acupressure

Spleen 6, also called The Gathering of the Yin-Feminine Energy, is a powerful point for stimulating and strengthening your female energy and reproductive system. To find it, sit down and cross one leg over the other so that your top leg is at a 90-degree angle. Do not force your legs if this is uncomfortable. Using your anklebone as a starting point, lay your fingers horizontally across your ankle area. Your pinky should be touching the anklebone. At the edge of your forefinger, you should feel another bone, located behind your shinbone. Press the tissue area on either side of this bone with your fingers and thumb until you find a slight soreness. Then use the same press-and-release pattern described in the previous tip. Switch legs and repeat. Another option is to sit in a lotus position and work on both ankles simultaneously. The sensation should be very soothing.

Make a Point to Increase Blood Flow

Spleen 10, The Sea of Blood, is another helpful point. When you are young, your reproductive cavity flows richly with blood. Although the blood flow decreases with age, stimulating this area may improve the microcirculation in your uterus, fallopian tubes, cervix, and your vagina. To find this point easily, sit on the edge of a chair or couch and place the palm of your hand on your thigh so that your middle finger is at the edge of your knee. You are looking for the point where your thumb hits on the side of your kneecap. Keeping your thumb on this point, straighten your leg, and apply pressure using the rest of your hand. Massage one leg and repeat the same steps on your other leg. When your circulation improves, so does your health and fertility.

Keep Your Immune System Strong

Large Intestine 4, Joining Valley, is one of the strongest and most commonly stimulated points in acupuncture. It strengthens the immune system and is also used to relieve headaches, menstrual cramps, and pelvic pain. This point is located between your thumb and your index finger. Open your thumb and index finger wide to see a V-shape. Press in the center of the V gently and hold for one minute on each side. Although this point is not specifically geared to stimulate your reproductive system, it helps adjust your nervous system to improve circulation throughout your entire body. Massage and stimulation can strengthen and revitalize you, and subsequently improve your fertility.

Chapter 6

Promote Pregnancy with Restoration, Spirituality, and Intimacy

Spiritual nourishment and stress management are just as important as what we feed our bodies. Inadequate rest, low quality sleep, and long working hours can all contribute to emotional instability. Your body detects if you are under a lot of stress and thus reduces your chances of getting pregnant. This is your body's protective mechanism; having a child requires a calm and healthy internal and external environment. Sometimes, becoming too involved in your active pursuit of pregnancy can also induce stress. As a result, your relationships may develop friction, causing depression, frustration, and eventually a dissatisfying social life.

Eliminating stress completely is very difficult, but it is very important for fertility potential that you make an effort to manage stress. One of the first steps you can take is to have a fertility treatment plan. This plan maps out the times for natural conception and any treatments you choose to incorporate. With the whole plan laid out, you are more organized, which helps decrease stress. Building a supportive network of friends, family, or relatives with whom you can talk to regularly is also very helpful. Consider joining an infertility group or seeing a therapist to release your emotions. Practicing creative art therapy and immersing yourself in an activity you love are other helpful ways to relieve stress.

The key to avoiding stress and improving chances of fertility is to keep a healthy balance in your life of activity and relaxation. As social creatures, it is important for us to foster intimacy with friends and loved ones whenever possible. However, it is also important to give yourself the time to develop a closer sense of your inner self, so that you can be clear in your purpose of motherhood. Inner understanding and personal strength will dispel conflict, helping you achieve the optimal state of health that is necessary for peak fertility.

First Do Some Soul Searching

Before taking the necessary steps to motherhood, you must look deep within yourself and examine why you want to be a mother. It is crucial to become conscious of your decision and to question if you have the proper emotional and monetary resources to take care of your child, especially if this is to be your first child. Don't allow the time pressures to act as your driving force to have a baby; many women want to have a child simply because they are getting older and feel that the chance is going to pass them by. If you feel old today, how will you feel when your child is five, ten, and fifteen? Take the time to search within yourself to prevent making any rash decisions. Take into consideration how pregnancy will affect your health in the long run. This initial soul-searching will create more awareness and allow you to make the decision that is most appropriate for you.

Affirmation for Fertility

Our thoughts can often manifest what we believe to be true. If you often doubt yourself and your fertility potential, you are resisting the possibility of becoming a parent. Before you embark on your journey to fertility, try the spiritual tool called affirmation. Sometimes we need guidance to help us affirm and strengthen our faith. Affirmation is also a reminder to yourself that your body is a microcosmic universe ready to release the energy, if only you cut through surrounding obstacles. Just as you feed your body healing foods, you can feed your body with healthy, nourishing mental energy. Instead of letting your thoughts run wild with anxiety, fear of failure, or frustration, repeat words that reinforce your purpose. You could say to yourself, for example, "I am a person of love, compassion, and integrity. I am clear in my purpose and my body is healthy." Repeating positive affirmations can actually suppress the cortisol that the adrenal gland releases in times of stress—decreasing your stress level and leaving you peaceful and calm. "The Golden Light" may be also used as an affirmation for fertility and can be found in the Workbook for Spiritual Development by Hua-Ching Ni. May it bring you peace and light on your journey to parenthood.

The Power of a Vision

Creative visualization can help increase fertility. Ancient cultures have practiced placing symbols of fertility all around to ensure a successful progeny. Studies show that both literal reminders and creative visualization can offer beneficial results. By surrounding yourself with images of babies and happy families or by engaging in visualizing yourself playfully with children, you are directly participating in increasing the odds of achieving your objective. Never underestimate the power of your mind!

Make Time for Rest and Relaxation

Smaller studies published show the association between relaxation and a boost in fertility. Stress can inflict havoc on our overall health, and can take a toll on our reproductive system. A tranquil state can decrease overactive stress hormones, which in turn may improve your chances to conceive. Give yourself a relaxing foot massage, listen to calming music, or induce inner peace with meditation and deep breathing.

Sweet Dreamzzzz

Are you getting enough beauty sleep? Countless studies demonstrate the association between lack of sleep and poor health. Getting enough good-quality sleep is essential for proper hormone function, digestive health, and increased energy. To prepare for pregnancy, try going to bed around the same time each night. This will establish a sleeping routine that will condition your body to fall asleep around the same time each night. It is best to be in bed no later than 11 pm to ensure a restful 8 hours of sleep. Can't sleep? Try journaling or gentle stretching a half hour before bedtime to induce the relaxation response.

Blue: The Color of Calm

Studies show that people who love the color blue tend to be even-tempered, cool, and no-nonsense. Even if this doesn't describe your personality, you might want to try creating more serenity around yourself with color. Blue is the perfect color for relaxation because it stimulates brain production of the feel-good hormones serotonin and dopamine. Imagine how you feel when gazing at the blue skies above or the vast blue ocean. Because of its peaceful energy, blue may help you fall asleep better. For a quick fix, cover your bed in a blue comforter—or go more drastic and paint your entire bedroom a dreamy blue.

Less Stress for Greater Fertility

If you are constantly turning on your body's survival state by inducing the release of adrenaline, the last thing your body wants to do is to get pregnant, which would simply lessen your chance of running or fighting for your life. While we are not usually chased by tigers in our everyday lives, deadlines at work or conflicts at home can turn on the fight or flight state, if stress is not managed. Among the most effective ways to reduce stress are meditation, tai chi, and qi gong. These Chinese mind-body exercises gently increase energy while releasing overall tension. Try the Stress Release Meditation: Breathe consciously, relax, and with each exhalation, say "calm" in your mind as you focus on relaxing each area of your body in sequence, starting from the top of your head and moving down to your toes.

Reduce Work and Work-Related Stress

Modern-day life encourages competition and burdens us with long work hours. This stress takes a toll on our bodies and may reduce your chances of pregnancy. Try to limit your working hours to no more than 40 hours each week with a commute of no more than one hour a day. A balanced work and social life, with plenty of time for yourself, is a way to have less stress so you can focus more on getting pregnant. Keep your equilibrium by leaving at least one night a week open for just yourself. While on the job, take five minutes a day to simply close your eyes and breathe deeply.

Don't Worry, Think Happy

Studies show that a typical woman has 60,000 thoughts a day, and 80 percent of them are negative. Imagine what this is doing to her body! Our subconscious mind often feeds our conscious thoughts, which affect our physical body. Healthy thoughts bring good energy to your body and a relaxed body is more conducive to fertility. Affirmations, meditation, and deep breathing are all excellent methods to help you foster calm and peace. Try the many CDs and books on meditation, relaxation techniques, and qi gong—or look for an instructor in your area for guidance. Something to consider is that your physical body also informs your mental thoughts. For example, when you smile for 30 seconds, you increase endorphin release and decrease stress hormones—even if you weren't feeling particularly happy to begin with. Remember to be good to yourself and your loved ones, while believing in the goodness of the universe.

Increase Intimacy

As social creatures, we thrive on proximity and closeness to family, friends, and neighbors. This sense of community fosters wellbeing and increases fertility potential. When you spend more time with your loved ones, you feel happier and closer to your inner self. Allocate time in your schedule to spend with your partner, family, and friends so you can feel more content and connected while increasing your chance of getting pregnant.

Chapter 7

Form a Fruitful Partnership with Your Doctor

While the tips and techniques in this book are effective, each person is unique and has individualized needs, which are best served by a powerful partnership with a knowledgeable physician. Therefore, when using traditional Chinese medicine to enhance fertility, it is a good idea to keep your Western doctor in the loop. Some of the most successful fertility results have come from an integrative approach that uses both Eastern and Western medical techniques.

Choose a doctor—or form a team of doctors—in whose personal character and philosophy of healing you respect and have confidence. Health care is based around you as an individual, so your practitioners should be professionals who are sensitive to your needs and can personalize your care. Tell your practitioner that you want to be informed and learn how to maintain health and wellness so that you can take a proactive approach to your health and fertility.

One of the first steps you should take on a proactive journey to parenthood is to have a preconception medical appointment. Making an appointment with your doctor or gynecologist will allow you to review your own personal medical history. Anything that could interfere with your fertility potential may be detected and treated through a series of standard tests and procedures.

No matter what results you may encounter during these tests, it is important to avoid any hasty decisions. There are now more options available than ever before, and it is a good idea to take the time to fully explore them before rushing to action in desperation. With that in mind, it is a good idea to make an appointment to see where your health and fertility are today.

Pre-conception Checkup: Ask Questions

Your first checkup is a good opportunity to inform your doctor of your past and existing health conditions, as well as family medical history. If certain conditions, such as diabetes, run in your family, you may be at risk during pregnancy. Make a list of questions and concerns to discuss with your doctor so that you can take the necessary precautions to ensure a healthy pregnancy. It is also wise to inform your doctor of your menstrual history, medications, lifestyle habits, such as smoking or alcohol consumption, and if you have any sexually transmitted diseases that may create fertility difficulties.

The Basic Fertility Workup

A fertility workup is suggested for women who seem to be experiencing infertility issues, but an initial workup is a good idea for any woman who wants to see where her fertility potential is today; these preliminary tests evaluate the whole reproductive system. Most of the initial tests for assessing fertility are familiar to women and include a pap smear, pelvic exam, and perhaps a vaginal culture. Also, a few simple blood tests can help detect any possible hormonal imbalances. A pelvic ultrasound will help your doctor detect any possible abnormalities or cystic structures on your ovaries and uterus that may interfere with fertility. Your doctor will likely check your thyroid gland for any abnormalities, as this could have a big impact on your fertility potential. These tests are a good starting place for a doctor to determine whether more tests are in order.

Possible Fertility Obstacles

A healthy woman that is in a healthy relationship and has regular unprotected intercourse has approximately an 85 percent chance of getting pregnant in one year's time. If a year has passed without pregnancy, there are many possible obstacles and reasons. If you have irregular menstrual cycles, are older than thirty-five, or have known diseases that could create conception difficulties, including tubal diseases, uterine fibroids, or endometriosis, it is essential that you and your partner immediately get an initial fertility work up with a health care practitioner who specializes in reproductive medicine. Additionally, it is important for the man to be evaluated by a doctor, because nearly half of the time, the male partner can account for difficulty conceiving. Standard semen analysis involves your partner masturbating into a cup and the analysis of the sperm content by a fertility laboratory technician.

Is Your Endocrine System in Harmony?

After the preliminary tests have been done, a doctor may feel that he or she needs more answers. The Western approach uses diagnostic tests to determine the cause of infertility. These tests focus on the main areas of the female anatomy, including the endocrine system, ovaries, cervix, uterus, and fallopian tubes. The first step to determine whether there is an imbalance in your hormonal system is to undergo a few blood tests. While there are many possible tests, some of the most common test your thyroid-stimulating hormone (TSH), follicle-stimulating hormone (FSH), prolactin (PRL), and your estrogen levels. Blood for these hormones is usually drawn on the second or third day of your cycle.

Test Your Progesterone Levels

Ovarian dysfunctions account for nearly 40 percent of infertility cases, but it is often very difficult to find the exact cause of the dysfunction. Many tests can be done to determine this, and one includes a blood test to measure progesterone levels in your blood to ensure that you are ovulating. Progesterone, an essential hormone produced after the release of the unfertilized egg (called the ovum), causes the lining of the uterus to thicken in readiness for the implantation of a fertilized ovum. By measuring these levels, your physician may determine the adequacy of this hormone in your blood. This test is usually performed a few days after your anticipated ovulation day.

Test Your Luteinizing Hormone Levels

Another test that is used to ascertain the cause of ovarian dysfunction is a blood test that checks luteinizing hormone (LH) levels. This test can help you determine when you are ovulating. LH increases significantly in your blood just prior to ovulation and can be measured in your urine. If you prefer, you may get an over-the-counter testing kit at your nearest pharmacy.

Sample Uterine Lining Cells

Ovarian dysfunction can also be assessed through samples of cells from the uterine lining. For pregnancy to occur, a healthy and sufficiently thick inner uterine lining is essential. A hysteroscopic procedure examines how a sample of this lining develops in response to growth hormones. This test can also indicate defects in the different phases of the cycle both before and after ovulation.

Get an Ultrasound of Your Ovaries

There is yet one more way to test the function of your ovaries. An ultrasound can inspect the number of maturing eggs and can show you whether or not ovulation is taking place. This is an important test because it may be able to identify a problem with the development of a follicle that would prevent normal ovulation. The two common types of ultrasound used are abdominal and vaginal. Unlike X-rays, ionizing radiation is not used. Instead, the ultrasound imaging exposes parts of the body to high-frequency sound waves in order to produce internal views of the body. It is used to show internal structure, movement of internal organs, and blood flow.

Chart Your Basal Body Temperature

Taking your basal body temperature (BBT) each day and charting the rise and fall through a menstrual cycle can give a picture of the overall functioning of your reproductive hormones; your bodily hormones can cause changes in your body temperature. A relatively inexpensive procedure, charting your BBT involves using a basal thermometer first thing every morning and writing the numbers on a chart. While physicians today use other tests to determine ovary function, measuring BBT during one complete menstrual cycle gives information about the function of the ovary, its follicular development, and the secretion of progesterone. Assessing the rise and fall for a few cycles shows an overall trend in your hormonal and ovulatory cycling, information which can detect subtle problems before they expand into bigger problems.

Examine Your Cervix, Uterus, and Fallopian Tubes

The cervix is usually checked during your initial pelvic examination. Tests for ascertaining the state of the uterus are hysterosalpingography (HSG) and ultrasound of the uterus. In HSG, dye is injected into the cervix, filling the uterus and fallopian tubes, and then an X-ray is taken that describes the size and shape of the uterine cavity and detects abnormalities that affect reproduction, such as fibroids or uterine polyps. An ultrasound of the uterus is used to diagnose fibroids and other factors that influence fertility. If however, your doctor isn't completely certain of what they see in your ultrasound, a hysteroscopy might be ordered. In this exam, a camera is inserted into the vagina and uterus to inspect the uterine cavity. This procedure can be used to detect and remove a polyp in the uterus, which can sometimes interfere with the implantation of the embryo. The health of your fallopian tubes should also be ascertained because they provide the most likely location for the sperm to penetrate and fertilize the ovum.

Traditional Diagnosis: Pulse, Tongue, and Face Reading

Most people don't realize that their face, tongue, and pulse provide information about what's going on beneath the surface. Your body speaks a unique language to communicate the imbalances within it. Chinese medicine has mastered the art and science of reading the body's language over its five-thousand years of practice. Through taking your pulse, looking at your tongue, and reading your face, I can usually tell what overall health issues may be affecting your fertility. You may wonder what I could possibly know from looking at your tongue or face! Blemishes on the side of your nose could indicate chronic stress, a pale tongue might suggest anemia, and a wiry, tight pulse during your menstrual cycle could be a sign of ovulation difficulties. After reading these subtle signs, I would also take into account your history and reference any conventional workups you may have undergone. This type of diagnosis is complex, and if you are interested in the subtle clues it can provide, I advise you to find a traditional practitioner that is experienced in this type of analysis.

Speak Up

In Western society, the norm is to believe that the doctor is always right. However, if you have undergone some or many of these diagnostic tests and you feel that anything is confusing, seems peculiar, or makes no sense, it is your right to have your concerns addressed. Keep a list of all of your questions and speak up to your doctor. Your doctor is your partner in health and should address all your concerns until you know what you are dealing with. Take time making any decisions based on your diagnosis. Fear and anxiety will not result in the best possible choices for your care and your future. Getting informed and being proactive about your own particular case is the key to sound decisions.

Appendix

Wellness Living and Infinichi Products

Powerful Herbs for Natural Healing & Prevention

Products are available on http://www.askdrmao.com/ or from Tao of Wellness' clinic locations.

In ancient times, long-lived Chinese sages attentively observed nature. Their tradition of spiritual and natural life science came to be called Tao, which literally means The Natural Way. Over the centuries, they developed and refined traditional Chinese herbology, acupuncture, qi gong, and many other dynamic practices of health and healing.

These early doctors of Chinese medicine believed that with proper nourishment, the body could avoid physical problems and repair itself in times of illness. To that end, they artfully combined herbs in synergistic formulations for achieving bodily and spiritual balance.

My father, Hua-Ching Ni, is heir to wisdom and experience transmitted through an unbroken succession of 74 generations of Taoist masters dating back to the Han Dynasty, 216 B.C. His knowledge comes from thousands of years of medical expertise passed down through 37 generations of Ni family traditional Chinese medical doctors. Through Traditions of Tao, Hua-Ching Ni has made these treasured herbal formulations available to assist you in building the foundation for your own positive development in your quest for better health and greater fertility.

We at Wellness Living continue to use a collection of food-grade herbs to provide healthy energy and heightened vitality. As a 38th generation doctor of Traditional Chinese Medicine, it is my pleasure to share our family tradition of life-enhancing herbs with you.

Wishing you the best of health,

Dr. Mao Shing Ni, Ph.D., D.O.M., L.Ac., ABAAHP

*These herbs should be used according to individual needs; I highly recommend you seek guidance and customized formulation from a licensed practitioner. Some herbal supplements may interact with drug medications. Consult with your physician before beginning any new health regime.

*Statements contained herein have not been evaluated by the food and drug administration. These products are not intended to diagnose, treat, cure or prevent disease. Always consult with your professional healthcare medical provider before changing any medication.

SUPPLEMENTS, ELIXIRS, AND CREAMS

ALLERGIES

Allergy - This herbal supplement promotes temporary relief from allergy symptoms, including nasal and ear congestion, sneezing, wheezing, drainage, itchiness, and watery eyes. It can also be taken as a preventive during allergy season.

ARTHRITIS AND JOINT HEALTH

Arthritis/Joint - This supplement promotes the healthy function of joints and relieves painful symptoms of arthritis. It is also helpful as a preventive formula for athletes.

Tonic Oil - This oil is excellent for massaging aching muscles and painful joints and is helpful for healing bruises. Add a few drops to tea for relieving minor throat irritations or add a small amount to water for a refreshing bath. Rub on the temples and behind ears for some types of headaches.

Collagen Support - Collagen Boost is a high-potency vitamin, mineral, glucosamine and chondroitin formulation for promoting joint flexibility and mobility while strengthening skin, joints, ligaments, and tendons.

Pain-Free Patches – (See Pain Relief)

BONE AND TENDON HEALTH

DuraBone - This supplement is blended with vital anti-aging and bone-strengthening Chinese herbs, providing a natural source of vitamins and minerals to help strengthen and heal bones and tendons.

Bone Health – As we age our bones can lose their density and that can lead to breaks and fractures. Keep your bones healthy with easily absorbed calcium and natural herbs to aid your body's natural health.

BRAIN HEALTH

Fire Core Element: The Heart and Brain Tonic - This supplement supports the heart and cardiovascular function. Super Clarity nourishes the brain, clears and focuses the mind, heightens the senses, sharpens the memory, promotes blood flow, and opens the cardiovascular system, bringing joy to the spirit.

Brain Boost - Brain Boost contains DMAE, a natural antioxidant produced by your body that supports healthy brain function and mood, providing nutritional support for acetylcholine and reducing the buildup of beta-amyloid.

CANCER CARE

Live Long, Live Strong: An Integrative Approach to Cancer Care and Prevention Book and Qi Gong Package - Combine the power of *Live Long, Live Strong: An Integrative Approach to Cancer Care & Prevention* book with the effectiveness of our *Qi Gong & Meditation for Cancer Support DVD.*

A must-have for anyone who is going through cancer treatment and the people who care about them, as well as cancer survivors and those who are interested in living a long life without cancer.

Berberine - Berberine is a compound naturally derived from plants, including goldenseal, barberry, Oregon grape and tree turmeric. Chinese Medicine has been using berberine for thousands of years based on its "harmonious distribution" ability to target illnesses within the cells while causing minimal side effects.

Natural Immunity - Natural Immunity capsules are high-quality nutritional supplements made from pure extracts of olive leaf, mushrooms, and echinacea. Encapsulated in an all-vegetable product that contains no animal substances.

Thymus Support - Thymus Support provides a comprehensive blend of immune-enhancing ingredients to boost the body's natural immune functions. It helps the body to maintain good health and to prevent disease. These nutrients assist in establishing the body's cellular immune system, activating the immune system, and making it more aggressive in defending the body from invading bacteria and viruses.

CLEANSING AND DETOXIFYING

Wood Core Element: The Toxin Expelling Formula - This supplement increases the ability of the liver to cleanse the body of internal and environmental pollutants and toxins, balancing the nervous system and relaxing the mind. Internal Cleanse is especially helpful for relieving irritability, congestion, tightness, spasm, bloating and cramping, constipation and hypersensitivity.

Home Detox Kit - Our Home Detox Kit can be very effective and help you to restart your body's own natural detoxification process. Complete with a Detox Tea, Detox Bath, Dry Brush, Detox Protocol and Cleansing Diet, you have a complete system to strengthen your body's natural defenses.

COLD, FLU, AND IMMUNITY ENHANCEMENT

Immunity - This supplement boosts immune function and supports recovery from cold and flu symptoms.

Metal Core Element: The Immune Enhancing Formula - This supplement provides herbal nourishment to the lungs and large intestine to promote strong immune function and recovery from disease. Perpetual Shield is especially helpful for sinusitis, allergies, asthma, laryngitis, colitis, upper back pain, and proclivity to colds and flu, as well as skin trauma.

DIGESTIVE HEALTH

Earth Core Element: The Digestion Formula - This supplement stimulates digestion, which in turn improves nutrient absorption, encouraging physical vitality. Abundant energy is especially helpful for lack of energy, excessive worry, poor digestion, ulcers, inflammation, diarrhea, constipation, bloating, and water retention.

Over-Hang Over - Indigestion, nausea, loose stools, fatigue, and headache are symptoms of a hangover. This herbal formula is useful for hangover, alcohol withdrawal, and food poisoning.

Digest - This supplement harmonizes the stomach and promotes movement of stagnant food. It is useful for indigestion, bad breath, and belching, and it is also helpful for gastro-intestinal influenza, acute gastroenteritis or acute exacerbation of chronic gastroenteritis, acute or chronic cholecystitis, gastralgia, and acute pancreatitis.

Super Probiotics - Probiotics give your body an extra boost of good bacteria to encourage balance, nutrient absorption and to keep your immunity in check. Our Super ProBiotics is a freeze-dried culture of lactobacillus acidophilus and lactobacillus bifidus colonies per potency to give you the extra digestive support you need. Added benefits of probiotics are reduced fatigue, healthier skin, balanced moods, and even added weight management.

ENERGY ENHANCEMENT

Earth Core Element: The Digestion Formula (See Digestive Health)

HAIR HEALTH

Hair Nurture - This formula, taken internally, nourish the hair follicles and promotes healthy hair growth.

HEART HEALTH

Fire Core Element: The Heart and Brain Tonic (See Brain Health)

Omega Support - Omega Support is a proprietary blend of polyunsaturated-free, purified whole-body fish oils that are extracted through cold-pressed technology in order to preserve freshness and limit unpleasant taste. A proper balance of omega-6 to omega-3 acids is necessary for a healthy body and proper function.

LIBIDO AND PERFORMANCE ENHANCEMENT

Spark Male: Performance Enhancement - This specially formulated herbal blend boosts the Yang, stimulates masculine energy, boosts endurance, and brings all the components of male sexuality into enjoyable and satisfying natural harmony.

Spark Male Rollerball Oil - Enhance your masculine senses and enjoy the powerful benefits of this custom blend that sparks feelings of passion and desire. Utilizes the power of essential oils, such as cinnamon, neroli, and cedarwood to awaken and arouse your body.

Spark Female: Libido Enhancement - This combination of warming herbs enhances circulation, kindles the fire, enhances the senses to liberate inhibitions, encourages intense focused interest, and unblocks energy for the enjoyment of natural feminine enjoyment.

Spark Female Rollerball Oil - Enhance your feminine senses and enjoy the powerful benefits of this custom blend that sparks feelings of passion and desire. Utilizes the power of essential oils, such as cinnamon, jasmine, and rose to relax and warm your body.

LONGEVITY AND ANTI-AGING

Five Elements of Health and Longevity - This supplement is a powerful whole-body tune-up, combining all the herbs from Super Clarity (Fire), Abundant Energy (Earth), Perpetual Shield (Metal), Enduring Youth (Water), and Internal Cleanse (Wood). This natural whole food combination of 44 traditional Chinese herbs promotes physical vitality, high tolerance for stress, strong immunity, a clear mind, suppleness of body, healthy appetite and digestion, proper fluid metabolism, and balanced hormonal function. It is the perfect synergistic complement to High Performance.

> "It is only through hindsight that I can appreciate how much more energy and endurance I have now due to Five Elements and High

Performance. I really enjoy having friends ask if I've discovered a Fountain of Youth."

– C. Slivinski, R.N.

Water Core Element: The Anti-Aging Formula - This supplement tonifies the body to reduce the effects of a stressful lifestyle. Enduring Youth enhances the root force of life and is especially useful for impotence, infertility, aging, and urinary/genital and reproductive problems affecting the kidneys, bladder, urinary tract, ovaries, testes, hormonal system, lower back.

"I first began taking Enduring Youth on the eve of my 42nd birthday. I noticed that within a few days my skin looked smoother, clearer, and more alive. Then my hair got shinier. I rely on it whenever stress of lack of sleep threaten to make me look my age."

– Patti Davis

Cell Protection - Cell Protection is a high potency antioxidant that contains all the known antioxidant factors including selenium, vitamins, enzymes, and enzyme cofactors.

MEN'S HEALTH

Prostate Support - A unique combination of natural herbs designed to support the healthy function of the prostate.

MOOD SUPPORT

Mood Elevation - This herbal formula is helpful for relieving sadness and mild depression and calming the mind. It can also be used for post-traumatic stress disorder and postpartum depression.

PAIN RELIEF

Pain: Soothes Pain and Relaxes the Muscles - This herbal formula is useful for relaxing muscles and soothing many types of pain including gastric pain, abdominal pain, traumatic injuries, headache, menstrual pain, and toothache.

Pain-Free Patches - Relieve your tired, achy, or painful muscles and joints naturally with Pain-Free Patches. Works directly at the point of pain to ease you back into your regular routine. Our all-natural blend of Chinese herbs creates a healthy alternative to pain relievers that carry an array of side effects and works with your body.

SKIN AND BEAUTY

Exquisite Skin: Nurture the Skin from Within - This supplement tones, nourishes, and lubricates the skin; it is useful for recovering from skin problems associated with acne, psoriasis, and eczema.

Infinite Beauty Trio - The richly-lathering cleanser effectively lifts away impurities, visibly replenishing and fortifying the skin. The shine-free day formula with luminescent pearl powder and broad-spectrum sun-screen surrounds the skin in a protective cushion of nutrients to hydrate and ward off damaging UV rays. The nighttime moisturizer, infused with an advanced cocktail of pearl powder and age-defense ingredients, works while you sleep to repair, regenerate and rejuvenate skin.

> "I had a very serious acne problem on my face. I work very late at night and it causes hormonal imbalances in my body. After using Traditions of Tao products my acne has gone. I look in the mirror every day and give myself a big smile."
>
> -J. Wu

SLEEP SUPPORT AND RELAXATION

Sleep - This herbal formula nourishes and relaxes the shen (spirit), and helps alleviate insomnia, anxiety, and mental exhaustion. It is also helpful for panic attacks.

Calm: For Calm and Relaxation - This supplement manages stress, calms the spirit, relieves restlessness, alleviates insomnia, and helps control over-thinking.

Tension Rollerball Oil - Using a blend of high-quality oils and herbs, our chi-moving formula brings your muscles a warm relaxing feeling mixed with a cool sensation that keeps you active and moving. This convenient rollerball application is easy to use.

Sleep Tea - Sleep is essential to our health and mental wellbeing, but so many people find good sleep elusive. Our delicious blend of special herbs is formulated to soothe your nerves, nourish your being and relax you into restorative sleep. This fragrant tea is a unique combination of floral herbs that will delight your taste buds and can be enjoyed throughout your day but best at bedtime.

Sleep Rollerball Oil - Our custom blend naturally relaxes the body and mind to reset sleep patterns and leave you waking refreshed. Apply generously to temples, back of neck, wrists or bottom of feet. When rolling inhale deeply to relax into sleep.

VISION HEALTH

Eyes - This herbal formula nourishes dry, tired, and blurry eyes.

Cell Protection - (See Longevity and Anti-Aging)

WEIGHT LOSS

B-Slim: Lose Weight Simply and Safely - These traditional Chinese herbs help decrease appetite, diminish cravings, reduce bloating, improve digestion and fat metabolism, regulate blood sugar, and gently relieve constipation. The effects of this supplement have been proven effective in clinical trials supervised by Dr. Mao Shing Ni at the Tao of Wellness.

> "With B-Slim, I've noticed that I can say that I don't want to eat sweets anymore."
>
> –M. Goldsmith

*B-Slim does not contain ephedra.

Weight Control Drops - Weight Control suppresses appetite, improves metabolism to burn more calories, and reduces sugar and lipid levels in the blood.

WOMAN'S HEALTH

Passages Plus for Menopause and PMS - Avoid hormone replacement therapy: This supplement promotes premenstrual and menopausal hormonal balance, mood equilibrium, bone and skin health, temperature regulation, and sexual vitality.

Natural DHEA - Natural DHEA boosts DHEA that is made by the adrenal glands in order to restore youthful DHEA levels and guard against premature aging while promoting general well-being.

Ovarian & Uterine Support - Ovarian Support is specially designed to provide a supplement of nutrients, vitamins, and minerals to support the hormones that are used by the ovaries. Strengthening female organs, promoting normal cyclic growth of the ovarian follicle, providing relief for PMS and menopause symptoms to aid in overall good health.

BOOKS, MEDITATIONS, AND QI GONGS

The Tao of Fertility: A Healing Chinese Medicine Program to Prepare Body, Mind, and Spirit for New Life by Daoshing Ni, D.O.M., L.Ac.,

Ph.D. and Dana Herko - An esteemed doctor who has helped countless women achieve their dream of having a child offers his program for enhancing fertility through traditional Chinese medicine (TCM). Dr. Daoshing Ni, descended from more than 70 generations of Taoist masters, has achieved renown among high-tech infertility specialists, TCM practitioners, and his many devoted patients. The Tao of Fertility is the first book combining a practical plan for conceiving using TCM with empowering Taoist principles that can carry you through pregnancy, childbirth, and beyond. Enriched by moving stories of women who became pregnant using TCM, this is a compassionate, comprehensive handbook. Structured according to a woman's journey to conception, this book includes:

- A questionnaire assessing fertility potential
- A 28-day fertility enhancement program
- Simple meditations and acupressure points to improve reproductive circulation and relaxation
- Guidelines for mapping your fertility using Chinese methods of diagnosis
- Information on how herbs and acupuncture can increase fertility
- Eating plans for pregnancy, postpartum, and breastfeeding.

Meditations for Fertility - Join Drs. Daoshing Ni and Kumiko Yamamoto as they guide you in creating a sacred inner space to nourish your inner fertile essence. This powerful tool to revitalize your fertility is based on their many years of clinical experience, as well as ancient Taoist tradition.

Qi Gong for Fertility - Join Drs. Dao and Kumiko as they demonstrate qi gong practices to enhance your fertility and restore your inner body/mind/spirit balance. This powerful tool to revitalize fertility is suitable for both men and women and is based on ancient Taoist tradition along with Dao and Kumiko's many years of clinical experience.

Made in the USA
Coppell, TX
13 June 2026

81270661R00059